NATURAL DISASTERS

FLOODS

Luke Thompson

HIGH interest books

Children's Press
A Division of Grolier Publishing
New York / London / Hong Kong / Sydney
Danbury, Connecticut

Book Design: MaryJane Wojciechowski
Contributing Editors: Jennifer Ceaser and Rob Kirkpatrick

Photo Credits: Cover © Mark L. Stephinson/Corbis; pp. 4, 5 © Reuters/Bob
Padgett/Archive Photos; p. 7 © Reuters/Stringer/Archive Photos; pp. 8, 9 ©
Kaehler/Corbis; p. 11 © Scott T. Smith/Corbis; p. 12 © Kim Heacox/Peter
Arnold; p. 15 © Rick Doyle/Corbis; p. 16 © Buddy Mays/Corbis; p. 19 © Index
Stock Imagery; pp. 20, 21, 23, 25 © Corbis; pp. 26, 27 © AFP/Corbis; p. 29 ©
Dewitt Jones/Corbis; pp. 32, 33 Courtesy of The Village of Freeport, Mayor's
Office; p. 34 © Lloyd Cluff/Corbis; p. 36 © N. Carter/North Wind; p. 39 ©
Joseph Sohm/Chromo Sohm Inc./Corbis

Visit Children's Press on the Internet at:
http://publishing.grolier.com

Cataloging-in-Publication Data

Thompson, Luke.
    Floods / by Luke Thompson.
      p. cm. – (Natural disasters)
    Includes bibliographical references and index.
    Summary: This book explains why floods occur, describes
the disastrous effects of flooding, and discusses methods of
flood prevention and control.
    ISBN 0-516-23369-6 (lib. bdg.) – ISBN 0-516-23569-9 (pbk.)
    1. Floods—Juvenile literature. [1. Floods] I. Title. II. Series. 2000
551.48'9—dc21

CONTENTS

In September 1999, Hurricane Floyd struck the East Coast of the United States. North Carolina was hit the hardest. The hurricane dumped more than 1 foot (30 cm) of rain in just one day. Interstate 95 was so badly flooded that 170 miles (274 km) of road had to be closed.

The National Guard used helicopters to rescue nearly 1,500 residents from the rooftops of their flooded homes. People waiting for help had to watch out for poisonous snakes in the floodwaters. In several towns, water washed out cemetery graves. Coffins floated down the streets.

The flooding from Hurricane Floyd damaged or destroyed 31,600 homes. Crop and animal losses totaled more than $1 billion.

This picture shows flood damage in North Carolina, one week after Hurricane Floyd.

FLOODS

Floods are one of Earth's worst natural disasters. They are also the most common. Floods can strike quickly, often without warning. They can happen anywhere—in mountains, villages, or major cities. Every year, floodwaters in the United States cause more than $4 billion worth of damage. They kill an average of 146 people in the United States, nearly twice as many deaths as those caused by tornadoes. In many countries, the number of deaths caused by floods is enormous. In Bangladesh, a small country in Asia, thousands of people die every year because of flooding.

Major floods can put thousands of square miles of land under several feet of water. They can cause mudslides and avalanches in mountain areas. Homes stay underwater for days. People run out of food and clean drinking water. People become ill from drinking or coming into contact with polluted water.

After a terrible flood in Bangladesh, people had to travel by boat to reach their homes.

Floods are very powerful. They can lift houses off their foundations. Just 6 inches (15 cm) of fast-moving water can knock you off your feet. Flooding is especially dangerous for drivers. Cars can get swept away or overturned in just 2 feet (61 cm) of water. Floods remind us just how powerful nature is . . . and just how helpless humans can be in the face of natural disasters.

CHAPTER ONE

RIVER FLOODS

In the winter of 1995–1996, the northwest United States experienced heavy snowfall. Then, in February, the weather turned very warm. The snow melted quickly, turning to water. The water rushed into rivers. At the same time, heavy rain fell. In just one week, huge amounts of water caused rivers in Oregon and Washington state to overflow their banks.

The rivers rose so quickly that they washed away roads and highways. Small towns were under several feet of water. Farmers lost thousands of cattle. President Clinton declared eighteen counties in Oregon and thirteen counties in Washington disaster areas. National Guard troops moved in to help the flood victims. Using sandbags, soldiers built emergency walls to hold back the water.

The flood knocked out power in many areas throughout Oregon and Washington. A radio

Floods in the state of Washington destroyed many roads and highways during the winter of 1995–1996.

operator in Woodland, Washington, risked his life to help give out information about the flood. "My house was under 4 feet [1.2 meters] of water," he told reporters. "But I went up to the top floor and kept broadcasting. It was crazy. Huge pieces of lumber were floating down the street."

Oregon officials estimated that the flood caused $400 million worth of damage to their state. Eight people died in the floods. Fifty more were injured.

Every river has a bottom, or floor. A river also has sides, or banks. Water flows along a river's floor and banks. This path is called a channel. Every river channel has a maximum amount of water that can flow through it. A river flood occurs when the amount of water flowing through a channel becomes more than the channel can hold. A river will then overflow its banks, causing flooding in nearby areas.

The Missouri River overflows its banks after a rainstorm flood.

RAINSTORM FLOOD

The most common reason that a river will overflow is too much rainfall in a short period of time. This type of flooding is called a rainstorm flood. Usually, rainstorm floods are a result of several storms. When a rainstorm hits an area, the soil becomes full of water. If a second rainstorm follows while the ground is already soaked with rain, there is nowhere for the new rainwater to go. This new rainfall

flows toward the nearest river. The river can't hold this extra water. The river begins rising. Water flows over the banks of the river onto the surrounding land.

SNOWMELT

A second cause of river flooding is snowmelt. In the spring, the weather becomes warmer. The winter snow thaws (melts). If an area has had a very snowy winter, followed by a quick thaw, there is a lot of snowmelt. This water runs downhill to lower-lying areas and to rivers. If too much snowmelt suddenly runs into a river, the river channel cannot contain all the water. Then the river spills over its banks and floods the nearby land.

ICE JAMS

Ice jams are another cause of river flooding. During the winter, rivers in cold areas freeze. In the spring, the ice softens and breaks into

Ice can break apart and float downstream, causing a river to overflow its banks.

chunks. These chunks float down the river. Sometimes the ice does not break up completely. These ice chunks are too big to move through the channel. The ice jams up the river, stopping its flow. First, the water that is held back by the jam overflows the river upstream. Then, when the chunks of ice thaw, the jammed water rushes downstream at high speeds. The river can't contain the rushing water, which flows over its banks.

WHEN DAMS FAIL

The worst river floods often occur when dams fail. A dam is a man-made wall that is built to hold back river water. Dams have floodgates that workers can open to release some water. Opening floodgates helps to release pressure when water builds up on the upstream side of the dam. Dams can only handle so much water, though. If rainstorms bring too much water, the water can force its way through the

When too much water builds up, the pressure may cause a dam to fail.

dam wall. Or, the water might get so high that it spills over the dam. Old dams can break under the force of too much water.

Dams usually are built upstream of towns and cities to prevent flooding. If a dam breaks or fails, the water can wipe out entire towns. In 1889, the South Fork Dam broke above the town of Johnstown, Pennsylvania. The dam had been used to make a lake for a country

*Deadly flash flooding causes huge amounts of water
to rush down the sides of hills.*

club. When the dam burst, a wall of water 20 feet (6 m) high flooded Johnstown. More than 2,200 people died in the disaster.

FLASH FLOODS

Mountains have many deep, narrow valleys. These valleys, or canyons, can flood suddenly during large rainstorms. Large storms can drop huge amounts of water in a short period of time. These sudden floods are called flash floods. Water starts rushing down the canyons. Flash floodwater can quickly get up to 20 feet (6 m) high. This rushing water carries with it mud, rocks, and trees.

DID YOU KNOW?

Geologists believe a gigantic, prehistoric flood formed the Grand Canyon. The Colorado River is what remains of this flood.

Flash floods are the deadliest kind of floods. Almost 75 percent of all the deaths that result each year from floods are because of flash floods. In 1990, 4 inches (10 cm) of rain fell on Shadyside, Ohio, in a two-hour period. The rain produced a 30-foot (9.1-m) wall of water, which flooded the area. The flood drowned twenty-six people and caused $8 million in damage.

CITY FLOODS

Most of the ground in city areas is covered with blacktop and cement. This paved ground cannot absorb any water. Rainfall and snowmelt must be drained. Cities build underground drainage systems, such as sewers, to collect the water. The sewers then move this water out of the city.

If there is too much rainfall or snowmelt, drains get backed up. Then the water has nowhere to go. Streets turn into rivers and parking lots become lakes. Driving becomes impossible. Water pours off roadways and sidewalks into subway stations. Subway tracks are submerged underwater, and trains can no longer operate. A huge downpour can bring enormous cities, such as New York City, to a complete halt.

Driving is impossible during floods, as motorists learned in New York City.

CHAPTER TWO

COASTAL FLOODS

On the morning of September 8, 1900, a deadly hurricane swept across the Gulf of Mexico. It battered the island city of Galveston, Texas. Storm surges (huge domes of ocean water) pushed ashore, flooding the coastal city. By noon, ocean water had flooded the entire waterfront. Streets and train tracks were under several feet of water. The flood washed away bridges that connected the island to the mainland.

The water rose so quickly that by early evening most of the city was under 15 feet (4.6 m) of water. Buildings, homes, and trees broke apart from the force of the floodwaters. Residents drowned as they tried to swim or outrun the fast-moving water. Many people were pinned underwater by wreckage in the rushing water.

This picture shows damage in Galveston, Texas, after the hurricane of 1900.

FLOODS

When the ocean water finally receded (moved back), most of Galveston had been destroyed. It is estimated that six thousand people lost their lives in the storm. Most of the damage and deaths from the hurricane were because of flooding.

Coastal flooding occurs when the level of ocean water rises. This rising water produces huge waves and storm surges. These waves and surges push large amounts of ocean water into coastal areas. Two types of natural disasters are responsible for coastal floods: tropical storms and tsunamis (giant waves).

Tropical Storm Floods

Tropical storms and hurricanes are the storms responsible for most coastal flooding. These storms produce high winds, heavy rains, and large waves. When tropical storms strike the coast, they dump huge amounts of water—

*Not even seawalls can hold back storm surges,
which lead to coastal flooding.*

often 6 inches (15 cm) or more—in a short period of time. Hurricanes also produce storm surges, which can measure from 50 to 100 miles (80.5 to 161 km) wide and more than 20 feet (6 m) high. These powerful domes of seawater crash into the shore and flood entire coastal areas. Storm surges drown people and wash away beaches, homes, and boat marinas.

Tsunamis

Coastal flooding also can be the result of tsunamis. A tsunami is a giant wave that is created by an earthquake or volcano in the ocean. During an underwater volcano eruption or earthquake, the ocean floor will suddenly break apart. Millions of tons of water are shoved upward. The force of this push creates a long wave, or swell, on the surface of the ocean. The swell moves across the ocean at a high speed. When the swell nears the shallow water of the coastline, it surges upward. This surge creates a tall wall of water that is known as a tsunami. Some tsunamis have measured 55 feet (16.8 m) high. When a wave that large hits the coastline, it can carry water several miles inland.

An enormous tsunami hits the coastal towns of Hawaii, flooding the streets of Laie Point, Oahu.

CHAPTER THREE

FLOOD DAMAGE

In December 1999, Venezuela was struck by the worst natural disaster to hit South America this century. Flooding and mudslides caused 30,000 deaths. More than 100,000 people were left homeless by avalanches of mud and rocks. These avalanches rushed down the sides of mountains, burying houses and people.

Dead bodies were trapped beneath mud and water. Some bodies floated off to sea. The bodies rotted in the open air because there weren't enough people to bury them. The bodies that were recovered were hard to identify.

Thousands of people were stuck on rooftops, waiting to be rescued by boat or helicopter. Many more people became ill from diseases carried by dirty floodwaters.

In 1999, flooding and mudslides destroyed a large area of Venezuela.

27

FLOODS AND DISEASE

Many of the deaths caused by floods are actually because of dirty, contaminated water. Water that is contaminated contains dangerous substances, such as germs and chemicals. Germs grow when sewage systems overflow into floodwaters. Drinking water and food become contaminated. Floods also can wash away chemical containers from farms and factories. These chemicals, such as pesticides, can be dangerous. People who swallow floodwater can get sick. People with cuts on their skin can get infections.

Mosquitoes grow in pools of water left behind after floods. Mosquitoes can carry deadly diseases, such as encephalitis and malaria. Hepatitis is another disease that can be spread by contaminated water.

After an October 1998 flood in Calcutta, India, a deadly disease called gastroenteritis spread throughout the city. More than three

After a flood, rivers can become polluted by chemicals.

hundred people died as a result of eating food contaminated by dirty waters. In December of that same year, a flood in Honduras spread a virus called *leptospirosis*. Rats from flooded sewers moved into the city streets. The rats spread the disease by urinating in the water supply.

PROPERTY DAMAGE

Floods are responsible for billions of dollars' worth of property damage worldwide each year. Millions of acres of farmland are destroyed every year by floods. Floodwater washes away crops and soil. When huge areas of farmland are destroyed, it hurts the whole country. Farmers lose money when their crops are wiped out. People who depend on these crops for food go hungry. In small countries that depend on these crops, whole economies can fall apart.

Floods damage homes and businesses, too. Houses are knocked off their foundations by

DID YOU KNOW?

The most expensive flood in American history happened in 1993. The Mississippi River spilled over because of rainstorms. Throughout the Midwest, 23 million acres of dry land were covered with water. In Iowa, floodwaters eroded (washed away) several feet of ground, exposing rock that was 375 million years old! Officials calculated the damages from the flood at $25 billion.

fast-moving water. Others can no longer be lived in because of dirty floodwater. Business owners lose machinery, records, and goods in floodwaters. Floods cause an average of $1 billion worth of damage each year in the United States.

AFTER THE FLOOD

Floods can happen very quickly, yet their effects can be felt for a long time. Land can stay covered with water for days, weeks, even months. Over time, however, floodwaters will recede. Rivers will return to normal water levels. Sea tides retreat as ocean storms die down. Water on the land eventually spreads to wider areas. The water finds soil that can absorb it. The sun heats up the floodwater, causing it to evaporate (turn from a liquid into a gas). Often the total damage—both in loss of lives and in property damage—cannot be determined until floodwaters have receded.

CHAPTER FOUR

FLOOD SCIENCE AND PREVENTION

Mary Klotsche had seen her share of coastal floods in her life. Her home in Freeport, on New York's Long Island, had flooded several times. She even had purchased a special machine to pump water out of her basement.

In 1986, while pumping out water during a flood, Klotsche had a heart attack. "I have heart problems," she explained. "Pumping the water out of the basement was never good for me." But she was so fed up with flooding that she kept on pumping. She didn't go to the hospital until the waters had died down.

In 1998, the village of Freeport decided to do something about its flood problem. Homeowners hired construction crews to raise their homes off the ground. Klotsche was one of the first to have her home redone. Workers raised her house 5 feet [1.5 m] off the ground. "It was like a tourist attraction when they

In Freeport, Long Island, houses were lifted 5 feet (1.5 m) off the ground to protect them from flood damage.

The Aswan Dam in Egypt prevents the Nile River from flooding.

raised the house," Klotsche said. "People came out to watch it. Now, when it floods, I can just watch the water flow by."

One of the reasons that floods are so dangerous is that so many people live near bodies of water. Much of the world's population lives in areas where flooding is likely to occur. Paris,

New Orleans, Rome, and Washington, D.C., are just a few major cities built on land that easily can flood. Areas that flood on a regular basis are called floodplains.

Scientists figure out where these floodplains are located. These scientists are called geologists. Geologists try to figure out ways to prevent floods. They also look for ways to reduce damage from floods.

DAMS

Geologists work with engineers (experts in designing buildings, bridges, and other structures), to make dams. When water levels rise, water builds up on the upstream side of the dam. Dam workers then release the water through floodgates at a safe rate to the other side of the dam. The Aswan Dam in Egypt is a famous example of this type of flood control. The dam has stopped the yearly flooding of the Nile River.

Sometimes dams are used to start floods. Dam workers let just enough water through the floodgates to create a controlled flood. No people are put in danger. Scientists study these man-made floods and collect information. Then they use what they learn to help prevent future flood damage.

PREVENTING FLOODING

Another way to prevent flooding is to increase the amount of water a river can hold. Engineers look for ways to allow water to flow

easily through a channel. They remove fallen trees, boulders, or anything that can clog up a river. They also design levees (walls) along riverbanks. A system of levees helped to protect New Orleans from floods during Hurricane Georges.

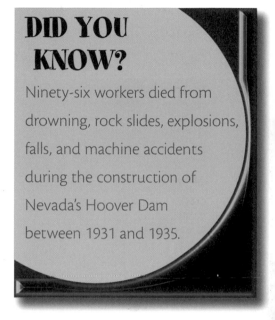

DID YOU KNOW?

Ninety-six workers died from drowning, rock slides, explosions, falls, and machine accidents during the construction of Nevada's Hoover Dam between 1931 and 1935.

To prevent coastal flooding, engineers design tall, thick walls, called seawalls. They use cement and metal to make the seawalls strong enough and high enough to protect areas from storm surges. After the Galveston, Texas, flood of 1900, engineers built a seawall that stood 17 feet (5.2 m) high. This seawall protected the city from flood damage when another hurricane hit the area in 1915.

Levees along the Mississippi River protect Midwestern states from floods.

FLOOD WARNINGS

Information about weather patterns helps meteorologists (weather scientists) to predict storms that can cause floods. Studying soil, rivers, and ocean tides also helps scientists to predict areas where flooding can occur.

The National Weather Service is a government agency that looks for possible flood weather. If this weather occurs, the agency sends out warnings on television and radio. The warnings inform people where and when a flood may strike. The warnings also tell people whether they should leave an area or move to higher ground. An early warning will give people more time to prepare.

FLOODING DO'S AND DON'TS

- Watch or listen for flood warnings during heavy storms.
- Do not try to walk, swim, or drive through floodwater.

*If a flood strikes where you live, you should only
drink or wash with bottled water.*

• Use only bottled water to drink, wash dishes, brush your teeth, prepare food, or make ice.

• Move important things in your house to a second story or attic.

• Stay away from power lines, especially if they are lying in water.

• If you have any cuts on your body, see a doctor about a tetanus shot.

Fact Sheet · · · · · · · · · ·

GREENLAND

NORTH
AMERICA

NORTH
ATLANTIC
OCEAN

SOUTH
AMERICA

PACIFIC OCEAN

SOUTH
ATLANTIC
OCEAN

The red areas on the map show where
extreme floods occurred in 1999.

1999 Extreme Floods

EUROPE

ASIA

AFRICA

AUSTRALIA

NEW WORDS

absorb soak up

bank the side of a river

canyon a mountain valley with a stream

channel the body of a river, made up of a floor
   and two banks

coastal flood flooding caused when the level of
   the ocean rises

contaminate to make something unclean or dis-
   eased

dam a large, man-made wall built to hold back
   river water

engineer an expert in designing bridges, dams,
   and other structures

erode wear down

evacuate to order people to leave an area because
   it is unsafe

evaporate to change from a liquid to a gas

flash flood a flood resulting from a large amount
   of rain in a short period of time

floodgate part of a dam used to release water

floodplain an area that floods regularly

floor the bottom of a river

geologist scientist who studies the Earth

ice jam chunks of ice that block a river's flow

levee a man-made wall built to strengthen a river-bank

meteorologist a scientist who studies the weather

National Weather Service a government agency responsible for observing and forecasting the weather

rainstorm flood flooding caused by too much rain in a very short period of time

saturated fully soaked with water

seawall a wall that protects a coastal area from the force of the ocean

storm surge a huge dome of ocean water produced by a hurricane

swell a long wave that travels over the surface of deep water

thaw the melting of the snow and ice in the spring

tsunami an extremely large wave caused by an earthquake or volcano in the ocean

urban having to do with the city

FOR FURTHER READING

Barber, Nicky. *Fire & Flood*. Hauppage, NY: Barron's Educational Series, Incorporated, 1999.

Drohan, Michele Ingber. *Floods*. New York: The Rosen Publishing Group, 1999.

Duey, Kathleen and K. A. Bale. *Mississippi, 1927*. Old Tappan, NJ: Simon & Schuster Children's, 1998.

Erlbach, Arlene. *Floods*. Danbury, CT: Children's Press, 1995.

Gross, Virginia T. *The Day It Rained Forever: A Story of the Johnstown Flood*. New York: Puffin Books, 1993.

Keller, Ellen. *Floods!* Old Tappan, NJ: Simon & Schuster Children's, 1999.

American Red Cross Disaster Services—Floods
www.redcross.org/disaster/safety/floods.html
The official site of the Red Cross provides information on floods, including what to do when flood warnings are issued and tips to help you prepare for a flood.

Coping with Floods
www.ag.ndsu.nodak.edu/flood/flood.htm
A page with information on flood preparation and flood recovery designed by North Dakota State University. It includes tips for keeping your home and food safe after a flood.

Federal Emergency Management Agency
www.fema.gov
This government-sponsored site shows areas that are in danger of experiencing floods or other natural disasters. It has advice about what to do you before, during, and after a flood.

Nova Online—Flood!

www.pbs.org/wgbh/nova/flood

This site of the popular public television series includes information about and pictures of floods. It also contains a history of rivers that are famous for flooding. There also are examples of the positive aspects of floods, such as how farmers actually may benefit from a flood.

U.S. Geological Society

807 National Center

Reston, VA 20192

888-275-8747

Web site: *www.usgs.gov*

This site includes government studies of past floods and predictions of future floods.

INDEX

INDEX

ABOUT THE AUTHOR

Luke Thompson was born in Delaware. He holds a degree in English literature from James Madison University. He lives in Vail, Colorado.